Agile Project Management For Beginners:

An Essential Scrum Mastery, Software Agile Development, Product Development Managing Guide

By

Joseph Joyner

Table of Contents

Agile Project Management For Beginners: An Essential
Scrum Mastery, Software Agile Development, Product
Development Managing Guide

By Joseph Joyner

First Published, 2015

Printed in the United States of America

Introduction

Agile Project Management focuses mainly on the value of the customers first. It is formed by a team who put more attention on the interaction of the team rather than accomplishing. They approach the reality of the current business rather than to plan and follow it. The Agile Manifesto's key principles and organizational practices is what Agile Project Management is based from. The Agile Project Management helps in giving high technicality and value even if you don't have the luxury or a big budget. The good thing is that the principles don't only refer to software development, but it also gives people a way of thinking towards management approach to be able to develop consensus quickly in an environment that is fast-paced.

Chapter 1. Scrum Basics

Scrum is the agile way of managing a project that usually concerns software development. The way that Agile software is seen as a form of methodology under Scrum rather than seeing it as methodology. It is like the framework that builds a process of management. It is the Scrum development that is assigned to do most of the project that needs to be accomplished rather than giving all of the details regarding the project. This process is done because they will be able to present it really well because they are the ones who made the project. The Scrum is reliant on a team that is self-organizing and self-functional. A scrum team is formed by a group of individuals with no leader who is supposed to just assign tasks. Instead, the team decides what to do in each aspect as a whole. A scrum team is said to be cross-functional because all of the team members are supposed to take the idea that they have and implement it. When talking about Agile development, there are 2 roles in the team. 1st is the Scrum Master who has the role of being the coach and the mentor of the team. They are also supposed to drive the team towards the right direction. The

Product Owner (PO) is the 2nd role and this role represents the customers in order to give the team a better outlook towards the direction they are supposed to be heading.

More will be discussed in the latter part of this book.

Chapter 2. Agile Project Management Advantages

Agile Project Management gives stakeholder engagement which means that it provides a lot of opportunities for both the team management and stakeholder through the whole process of time-boxed sprint. This allows the client to get involved in the steps to take for getting the project done right. This entails a lot of interaction and collaboration for the project team and the client. This will also help the team in finding out what the client wants. Since every step is give a time-frame, the client will be able to see clearly that the work is progressing. The team gets more trust from the stakeholder because they have shown their abilities in giving software that is of high-quality because they will be able to see physical results. Since the clients are clients are involved in making the project, they are also able to see the transparency of what is being done. It lets them into the process of planning the project, reviewing, and software building that will have new features. The client in return should be able to understand the progress of the work that is happening so that they will have transparency through the whole process. During the project management process, the team will put a schedule of 1 to 4 weeks in the time-boxed duration to iterate new features and give a level of predictability that is high and achievable. This can also open the opportunity to try releasing beta software earlier than planned. This provides early and predictable delivery for the project. The time-boxed iterations in the schedule will give the team the prediction about how much work is possible to be done in a given time and the cost per iteration. They will estimate and give the client the cost before proceeding with the next iteration. This will help the client in deciding about each feature because they will know the approximation that will be added in every iteration. This gives the client predictable costs and schedule.

After the cost has been given an approximation for all iterations, the team can still make changes to polish, refine, and what needs to be prioritized more based from the backlog of the product. If there are backlog items that need to be changed or added, they can be discussed and planned for the succeeding iterations, but allowing change in the coming weeks. By focusing on the business value, the client will be given the permission to determine what needs to be prioritized more regarding the features and can deliver them in an order that is valuable. The Agile mostly stories together with an acceptance criteria that are business-focused in order to define the features of the product. Since the team focuses on what the customer needs, each feature will give values incrementally and not just composed of IT. This will give a chance to beta test the software after finishing every iteration. By doing this, they will be able to know what needs to be changed basing from feedbacks so they know what needs to be improved because they are focusing on the customers. After the project has been thought through with the combined efforts of both the team and the client and guiding every iteration, the team will now have to room to focus on developing it into something that is of high-quality, testing, and a more effective collaboration. When there are builds that are being done frequently and also reviews after finishing every iteration, they will now be on their way to improving quality through determining what needs to be fixed in this stage of the process. They will also be able to find out what mismatches have been done earlier.

Chapter 3. Agile Project Management Issues

There are many Agile Project Managements that fail and it actually challenging to determine how many of them have failed because it is a lot. Most of them ending up not totally complete even though they say it is already complete. This can be due to the fact that they too much time in building it and the quality was not good. There are also some cases wherein the client was not entirely satisfied and the project ended up costing more than expected. There are 5 most common problems that occur within an Agile Project Management team and if not addressed quickly, can make the entire project fail.

1) Not having a product owner is one of them because no one will be there to make concrete decisions that need to be done for the project to become successful. Regardless if you are following the path of Scrum or your own style, a product owner is needed to give input so that it will lead the team towards the right direction. This is just like having your house remodeled. A group of people will come to you, but no one will be there to actually give specifications on

how the house should look, the colors, design, and others. You need to have someone who will be able to have a vision and create a beautiful design for your house. You will just end up wasting your money because no one was there to has the proper expertise to guide the process. There also instances when the team is not actually able to perform any real iterations. Iteration is to develop a certain product by making little steps. It is better to say that it involves the development of the product. It is like the proven concept of microevolution because microevolution pertains to the development of something over time adding up to something big in the future. This was best demonstrated by the evolution of the creatures that have living for millions of years, but they are not as evolved back then as they are today. The features of the project should be improved over time and it should not be forced to happen in one sprint or iteration and then move on to the next so you are actually not iterating.

2) Another issue with Agile Project Management is you are not breaking the things into pieces that are small enough for the team to accomplish. You need to be able to do this well to prevent procrastination from

happening because if they are not broken small enough, it can overwhelm the team and they will have no idea what to do next because the next steps are simply too hard. If the big project is showed in smaller parts, it will be easier to accomplish and it enables a clear vision of the progresses that are happening. Sometimes the person who is doing the backlog work is not thinking about all of the things involved in the work before asking the team to tackle it. These kinds of backlogs are hard to estimate because they are very large and it will take a lot of time to explain it to the team because they could not understand it well enough. Those who make these backlogs could repeat what they have submitted and break them down into smaller steps. When receiving a backlog such as this, give it back so they can fix it.

3) Lack of giving criteria for each backlog to tell when they are done is another problem that can cause a project to fail. If there is no one present to say whether the certain backlog or not, the team will not know how it should be when it Is done. They will just end up running out of time and that's when they say it is done even if it is still incomplete. If criteria were set, they will know how the backlog should be when it is done.

Better results will be achieved if you tell them concretely what you want. You do not want a backlog that is just enough, you want something that is done. This is like having a building built, but the paint has not yet been placed when the time runs out. You will say that the building can be used without paint because there are already walls, but the building will look ugly as the result.

4) The last major issue that makes a project fail is if you do not let the team be autonomous. You need to let them be a team no matter what your political persuasion is. This is like a country coming to invade another country and they will build a government that was not elected by the people to rule over them. This will cause a lot of problems. This is not letting the team have no accountability, but if you want a software project, you need to let them collaborate, manage, and organize themselves even in a small level. You will see that the team will learn to develop their roles, leadership, and cadence. If someone from the outside will try to interfere with what they are doing directly about how they are going about things, they will like they are not left on their own to decide what to do, they will think that they need to be careful. This can

pose as a threat to them which is why it might affect their progress. Teams work together, they expect that they will be allowed to discuss things on their own and trust will be placed upon them. They will not make any move that is not approved by the client so they should be given enough respect and trust. This is an issue that makes some projects fail because they feel like they are not capable enough to think on their own and provide ideas in making the project succeed on time.

Chapter 4. Agile Project Management Principles

Many have written about the benefits of the Agile Project Management in a team, but there are principles behind it that help guide the thought process of each individual who is part of an Agile Project Management team. When these principles are followed the implementation will also be successful in completing the project and making it ready for the customers to enjoy.

Principle 1 – To satisfy the customer through early and continuous deliver of valuable software

This is the most important thing because the purpose of the project is to satisfy those who will be using the software. When this is put into mind when doing a project, the team will not let anything stand in their way. They will become more efficient in doing their job because they are thinking of the customers who will be using the software. If users are prioritized, it becomes a motivating factor for the team to strive harder be lead in the right direction.

Principle 2 – To welcome requirements that will be changing, even those that are late in development. The process of Agile harnesses change to give competitive advantage to the customer

The methodologies regarding project management and software development that are linear usually do not like the idea of change. Even if this is the case, there is no such thing as a project going from the start to finish without experiencing any changes along the way. The Agile Project Management knows this fact and they find opportunity in it for the product to turn into something that the client truly wants or those who will use it. It will increase its ability to become more useful and satisfy the users.

Principle 3 – To deliver frequently software that is working with a time frame of a couple of weeks to a few months, but preferring to deliver it on a shorter period of time

The earlier methods of software development would focus on large amounts of documented information and data, but not really giving 100% of the requirements that were needed to complete a certain project. What really happens is that after spending a couple of months, you will have a lot of thick and very nice documented files, but there is really nothing there. Agile Project Management will focus on having working software frequently. There will be no delays and incompleteness.

Principle 4 – The developers and business people who are involved in the project need to work on it daily

It is important that the developers and business people work on the project daily. This will help in maintaining the agility and the ability of the software to have developments so it can keep up with the changing demands of the market. This concept is not known to those who have bene doing software development, but have not experienced Agile Project Management. This idea needs to be implemented, learned, taught, and be reinforced every time there is a project that needs to be done because it does not occur naturally.

Principle 5 – It aims to build the projects among individuals who are motivated. The environment and support needed needs to be given. They should also be trusted with the job

This means that micromanage does not work for Agile Project Management teams. There is no one better to tell the team what should be done than the people who are in the team. They understand the process more and if someone from outside tries to give an input, they have the option to consider it or not. They need to be allowed to decide on their own and figure out what must be done to keep the project moving. There is an Agile Project Manager who will be present to let them get their job done.

Principle 6 – Face to face conversation is the most effective way to deliver information efficiently

Face to face conversation is still believed to be the most effective way of conveying message because it is more personal than e-mails, text messages, and other forms to communicate with people. These technological advanced have made communication easier, nothing beats face to face conversation to convey what you really want to say.

Principle 7 – To measure progress, working software should be seen

This makes you think that this is a very easy thing to measure, but in reality, the open bugs, velocity of bugs that are being fixed, closed bugs, how many house are remaining on the project, how many hours have been spent on the project, how much has been spent, etc. are the things that need to be measured. These are the overheads that are needed in order to make software run smoothly. That's when you need to measure.

Principle 8 – Agile processes will be able to promote development that is sustainable. The sponsors, users, and developers should be able to give a steady pace for good

Back in the day, software development and those that are not a very agile project development methodologies would work extensively during crunch time when the schedule of the project is ending. This happened within the last 2 to 3 days before the project has to be given and only 2 to 3 weeks to go for working on the project. Everyone would rush and work overtime to complete the project on time which is not a sustainable way of doing a project. This kind of habit would cause health problems and other issues to those who are working on the project.

Principle 9 – Keeping attention towards technical excellence and creating a good design will enhance agility of the project.

This pertains to the fact that people should take pride in what they are doing. It's not all about hacking to give different codes in order to produce a sub-standard product. These developers use a tool called scrum and they give time in reviewing their solutions, find out what the best approach is so that it can be implemented. Their Agile Project Management Plan is developed into something that has a vision towards where they want the project to go.

Principle 10 – Simplicity is the art of being able to maximize the work done is important

This is to make a complicated task easier to accomplish so that everyone who is involved in making the project will fully understand what needs to be done to make the project successful. This is something managers want to see in their employees in the corporate culture. They want to see that their employees are busy even if the task they are working on is very simple. Simplicity should be implemented even in the corporate world to not make things too complicated for employees.

Principle 11 – Self-organizing teams deliver the most excellent requirements, architectures, and designs

Teams that are working under Agile Project Management work best when they are self-directed. There is a contradiction between those who act like they know it all and implements hierarchy to letting a team be able to contribute to the solution. When a team is self-organized, everyone is allowed to offer their own ideas, solutions, architectures, requirements, and other regarding the project to arrive at the best possible solution.

Principle 12 – During regular intervals, the working team will be able to reflect on the effectiveness and then adapt its behaviors accordingly

Learning to inspect and adapt is one principle of Agile Project Management that is being embraced. If a certain has been done like that for many years, it does not mean that it has to be done the same way today.

The team should be constantly trying to find out if it is only the solution and they should be able to come with a different solution that is more appropriate for doing something. If a new solution needs to be done, the team should adjust and implement that one instead.

Chapter 5. How Agile Project Management Works

The scrum framework is what makes up the heart of Agile Project Management. This involves using of meetings, events, roles, and increments to finish a product that is usable within a given time frame.

1 The product owner- This is the most knowledgeable one about the project being worked on and he/she will be the one to represent key stakeholders, end users, and customers. They are the one who is supposed to prioritize and fund the project. They should also be the one to describe how the final will become useful and will be able to speak to what the customers need to lead the team into coming up with the right product. Scope creep is also combated by the expertise of the product owner.

2 Scrum master – They are the ones who are in charge of the process management. The scrum master is the one who will be the problem solver so the product owner can easily drive the development of the product and to get the most out of their return on investment. The scrum master should make sure that every sprint needs to be self-contained and will not go through objectives that need to be added. They are also able to oversee the communication so that both the team and the stakeholder will be able to clearly see the progress that has been done.

3 The team- They are the group of individuals who are able to make requirements become functional. The project will be worked on by the team using sprints which are phases of work that are short which bring complete, documented, tested, and products that are functioning to their last part of development. If there is a new sprint that needs to be done, there will be a meeting and the members of the team will collaborate on what they will be able to deliver in a given amount of time. They will figure out what the goal is and assign tasks to team members to deliver the project successfully.

The Agile Project Helps by creating a team of people who are able to collaborate and perform tasks that are geared towards the completion of a certain project by doing sprints for every step and development of the project. With this kind of approach to projects, the outcome will become more appropriate to what the client wants and the end users will be able to enjoy.

Conclusion

Agile Project Management was created to help clients to be able to become more involved in the development of their project. They will be able to give their input, ideas, architecture, requirements, and vision to accomplish a project successfully. Even if this does not work for some people, there are still more product owners who try this approach because they want to be active in their own project and be able to collaborate with a team of people who will be working towards a common goal. By making sprints, the projects will be done more successfully because bigger tasks are broken down into simpler concepts so that the team will be able to understand what they will be doing.

This is a good approach if you are someone who will be confident enough to let a team handle your ideas and you should also be open to changes. You will see that the project is slowly evolving into something bigger that you want. If you have the right ideas and you are able to deliver your requirements well so they can work on it, you will have a good outcome. Make sure that you will not give complicated milestones that the team will have a hard time handling. You should also be ready to fund the project because there could be changes along the way which will require you to spend more, but it will be for the success of the project. Good enough is not the best way to go and you should continue to become more open to refinement of the project so that you will not be disappointed and have a good return on investment.

Thank You Page

I want to personally thank you for reading my book. I hope you found information in this book useful and I would be very grateful if you could leave your honest review about this book. I certainly want to thank you in advance for doing this.

If you have the time, you can check my other books too.

www.ingramcontent.com/pod-product-compliance
Lightning Source LLC
Chambersburg PA
CBHW070907070326
40690CB00009B/2030